GW01425386

The T
Teenage Mind

Ryan Bremner-Wright

BookLeaf
Publishing

India | USA | UK

The Truth of the Teenage Mind © 2024
Ryan Bremner-Wright

All rights reserved.

No part of this publication may be
reproduced, stored in a retrieval system, or
transmitted, in any form or by any means,
electronic, mechanical, photocopying,
recording or otherwise, without the prior
written permission of the presenters.

Ryan Bremner-Wright asserts the moral
right to be identified as author of this work.

Presentation by *BookLeaf Publishing*

Web: www.bookleafpub.com

E-mail: info@bookleafpub.com

ISBN:9789358318180

First edition 2024

DEDICATION

Jessica—for all your wisdom, honesty and encouragement.

Mum—for supporting me throughout life.

Grandma and Pops—for believing everything I've ever written has potential.

PREFACE

The tales in this collection are fictional representations of the inner feelings millions of young people endure during their progressive years. Some of the tales come from a personal space in my mind and allow me to reflect on the time I had as a teenager, whilst some of the tales come from the interactions I've witnessed. I wanted to give young people a voice... those who worry about, and fear repercussions from, their emotions, actions, and mindsets... I want them to be heard.

the first day

tears form at the back of my eyes
little ripples in the ocean
joining the rock at the back of my throat

currents surging
in the back of my mind
uniting irregular breaths

swirling greyness mixes
corrupted halos above
master's head—smiles are dead

corridors stretch into abyss
footfalls disappear, submitting
to the vacuum. waves

begin to grow—surging higher
the rock, a boulder now, sharp
coarse, splintering speech

singular sprains in glass
enough to make the foundations
tremble, quiver

blackness arrives ... tsunami
beats the barriers—silence—
corridors envelope me

what do i do?

the sonnet to anxiety

i am finding it rather hard to breathe
there are many faces glaring at me—
consuming me. a blackness—i can't see
the door—shrinking with glares—no way to
leave.
eyes are my nightmare nemesis. i swim to free
myself away from the glares and stares to be
my… self—not you. me! relieved to believe
that glimmers can be discovered in night
when hope seems extinguished—seize my
voice—
shout, cry, yell, scream my truth. show them my
fight
make them see me…for me. give them the
choice
to turn from nightmares and join my daylight.
learn the world is different. time to rejoice.

the daydreamer

why does it wait to rain on a weekday
whilst the sun belts through the blackening
blinds of my classroom
think of all the things i could do if the sun
graced us on a saturday
i love saturday
but not when it rains
my teacher would say it's pathetic fallacy
or something
pathetic
what a strange word
who called the weather pathetic when it's
powerful
not like a storm or a superhero but still
powerful
i hate superman what a waste of power
batman's cool

batman likes rain though well i think he does
suits his dreary backstory
i suppose that's a metaphor or something you
know what
i could be good at english if i could focus more
oh it's started to rain fantastically
i can hear it tapping no drumming behind the
blinds
i wonder what it's like to be in a band
fame celebrity fortune power greed joy
happiness unpredictability freedom
they wouldn't have to worry about what day it
rains

the gossip-er

silence can be cruel,
some drown in the
flood of nothingness—
some lustfully ravage
peace—satan's solitude

puppeteers string language
churning out deceit
a pantomime of lies
in a theatre for
beelzebub and mephistopheles

rest is not easily
found behind the envious
words of the puppeteers'

tongues whilst gluttony gorges
on the woeful sighs

tongues tie themselves
tightly around satan's
malicious vocals—covetously
plucking emotions, freshly
peeling tears from eyes

marlow's stage falls open
for faustus' submission to
satan's pleasure—pride
absorbs sorrow
sowed onto the concrete
grounds of the playhouse

tongues mould minds,
corrupts souls—wrath
inflicts pain…
scythes for sloth-like devils
dedicated to sacrificing innocent lives

in marlow's theatre
words hold power and
peers (the devils) feed
off written dialogue…
the lies and the ignorance.

the influencer

#prettyinpink
#muscleandabs
#newclothes
#travellyf
#seetheworld
#watchmylife
#freejourney
#sunseahappyme
#lookatwhatihave
#dowhatiwant
#iamme
#loveme
#noticed
#desire
#desperate
#seemeforme
#findmeplease
#doyoulikemeyet
#wontsomeonenoticeme

the fear

why can't people see
behind
the masks i wear
to hide
my worry
the mask that sheds
ageing and decaying
people recognise it
my soul
time lies a thick frost
strangling

the girl

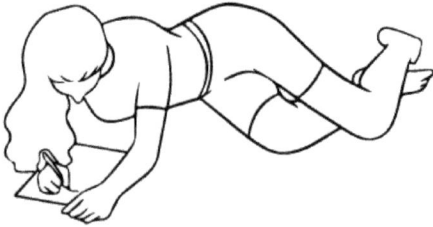

loving
you
makes my stomach
ache
grumble with nerves
tremble with excitement
quiver with anticipation

will you still love me tomorrow…?

the boy

loving
you
makes my head
lost
throb with panic
pound with ecstasy
thump with desperation

will you still love me tomorrow…?

the chameleon

…today i woke up
deciding to be different…
searching my wardrobe
for a new skin to wear…
following the shedding of
my redundant fragile shell…
no one can guess what i'll be
today but i know i'll be refreshed…
and remain invisible just like yesterday…

the torn

they argue who wants me more
between them both yet
they seem to ignore every word
torn
neither see my pleas for help

friends are blind to my pain
shadowed behind my eyes
not one
understands strains
struggles
of being split in two

watching every nuclear state
whilst i implode on myself
frightened
to declare
i'm nearing meltdown

'you
can get two of everything'
is not as comforting as
possessing what friends take
for granted
unity
i'm stuck between them as
the ring bell tolls
over me
'they both must love you
a lot' can't fade the guilt in my chest

'two birthdays' 'two christmases'
what's to be jealous
about a person who questions
themselves to sleep
desperate
to discover where they belong

my only thoughts
'was it my
fault'
'why can't they
love me together'

the sufferer

there's no enjoyment
staring death in the face.
watching its mouth twist
smirk into cackle
whilst the drops
from my wrists
paint my bedroom floor.
death doesn't give me sympathy
doesn't give me mercy
neither does the severing
slash of the blade.
death is relentless
buried in the front of my mind
every day strolling the corridors
ceaselessly stalking my shadow
its manacle claws twitching stretching towards
me
there's no enjoyment in staring death
in the face everyday
but i'm desperate to find

peace at the tip
of the
blade.

the repressed

'get a grip mate!'
'shake it off!'
'what you cryin' for?'
'man up...'
'you actin' like a girl for?'
'boys don't cry'
'don't be so gay'

... are people surprised we suffer silently?

the lost one

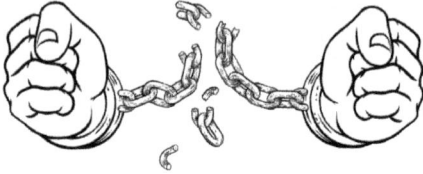

discovery depends on grit
i've spent too much
time in the light
comfort arrives in darkness

battling between jekyll
hyde consumes purity
a fog suffocating
daylight as my heart

pleads to escape chains
fortified
imprisoned

peace shouldn't need a
war before it
arrives

the new first dayer

joining—middle of the year
hoping to be free from my past

lights on my journey all sang green
chirpiness behind the bleating beeps

classrooms, like christmas toys,
sit expectantly, eager for me

walls don't cry here, don't shed here
perhaps time hasn't stolen them yet

warmth sweeps down my throat
cleanliness wrapped its arms around me

tables, varnished, silk smooth, glitter
twinkle under lights—stars on my path

what if my past catches me again?

the non-speaker

sometimes silence soothes the dread whirling in our heads. sometimes silence provides the peace so desperately craved. when the world's spin grows ruthless and noise plagues the ecstasy once had,
silence cures the throbbing pain raging, untamed and untethered, inside. the inferno tears away the tranquillity cradled for so long—the vortex of danger and damage and destruction, torments and
strangles the calmness. so, silence can become the saviour. sometimes silence suffocates the flames. sometimes silence chains the untameable. sometimes silence delivers peace.

sometimes silence wins.

the lover

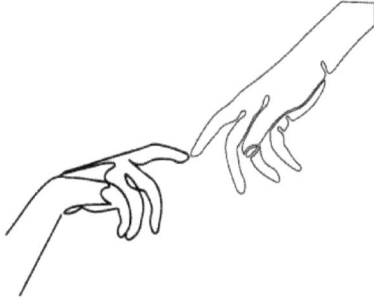

we've watched people fail,
crumble under the weight
of envy's expectations—
pressures.

we've overcome every
obstacle clinging to the
joyful tears we've shed.
together.

we can't be destroyed by
these talking, bitter walls—
we forbid its power, letting our hands
meet.

and my heart blushes
everytime.

the first kiss

stars sewed into the velvet blanket
pinned above our heads.
breath becomes shorter, sharper,
stolen by winter's grip.
we'd talk; ramblings
whilst constellations hummed over us.

your eyes sparkled that night
glittering like the frost settling
beneath our feet. we don't feel
the chill—a fiery warmth
explodes—a supernova of emotion—
the birth of a new world.
just us.

the breakup

at the beginning
the stars beamed upon us.
spotlighting joy spreading between us—
it's fluctuating, stagnating, dimming.
supernova burning out—colourful palette
drying up, dusty and grey.
explosions are intermittent, desperately
reinvigorating the exploration of our passions.
power sapped. i've never witnessed a dying
supernova before. hearts sinking, drowning
under the façade of a false love.
now we let each other walk
away into the velvet blackness which
used to cradle us.

the shapeshifter

the skin i wear only lasts
a few hours
once it expires
it's best before
it sheds away
leaving me naked lost
vulnerable scared
my wardrobe flooded
staleness trends
whatever is chosen
doesn't last long before
the expiry sets in
again
why can't my skin
be what i want

the pessimist

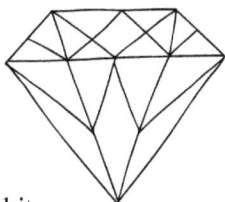

targets can't be hit
when their bullseye is a
touch off centre
and
stars can't be reached
when they're sewn a fingertip
out of touch
and
diamonds can't be formed
when the elements lack
purity
and
immortality is fragile
and
power weakens
and
idolisation churns out ugly
traits trampling esteem
and
i am nothing
i am worthless

the wanderer

often i just walk
lacking purpose
lacking quality.

often i just walk
hoping an end
will swallow me whole.

the memory

remember being at a party—i think
remember glass, glitter-balling on the floor—i
think
remember blackness beginning to swarm—i
think
remember friends shouting, warning—i think
remember plastic cups, slippery and sticky—i
think
remember blackness growing thickly—i think
remember voices goading, persuading—i think
remember actions, laughter, hating—i hesitate
remember eyes locking and holding... flirting—i
panic
remember hands—pushing, pulling... hurting—i
ache
remember blackness engulfed—i lost
remember later; ashamed, repulsed—i fear
remember the night, stained by bruises—i cry
every second; they don't believe—i remember

the discoverer

a voyager of my own skin
condemned to face the krakens
in my soul. fate
won't ever release me from this
shipwreck shell i'm encased
forever. my compass' magnetic
pulse beats uncontrollably
leaving me
isolated in a swarming rage
of fire and envy.
i suffered in my awakening
drawn into a battle of solitude
silence and repression.
no one lets me alone.
no one lets me alone.
no one lets me awaken; float.
life drowns.

the realist

these years are your fairytale.

but darkness lurks in
fairytales filled with goblins
and demons
facades of knights and princesses
failing to arise when times ring out
time is but a construct in fairytales
taken, manipulated by the spinster
twistedly succumbing to powers
formidably corruptible formidably dark
these years are your fairytale
this fairytale fails to give me my glass slipper
i live constantly at midnight

the prom king

legacy confirmed.
status cemented.
the crown perched
on my head settles
like the calming
winds after a storm.
passions. power. popularity.
i've had it all.
now it's correctly
recognised.
i reign supreme.
my subjects snap me
in my glory.
next a melody to
knight my coronation.
i made it here
myself. i expect
to be remembered.

the prom queen

years have passed
silver gold never
struck my mind
plastic crowns for
plastic people
i don't want it but
cheers engulf the room
eyes at the back
tell the real tale of
my time here.
flaws, faults, fatalities
clawing my way
topping the social mountain
now i want nothing more
than to hide away
from the glitterballs
thousand eyes burning
my skin
there's a more deserving
monarch than me
i pray i haven't terrorised them
into isolation.

the last day

i've spent most of my
school life waiting
for the world to open and
swallow me whole.
most of the time i've
stood patiently at the side
line watching others make
fools out of me.
most of the time i've
tangled myself in a
film of darkness, eager
for the journey to end,
to find comfort in the
knowledge i'll never be
cocooned by parasites again.

strobes of light dance
from within the envelope
my heart brightens, burns, pounds,

explodes realising freedom was around the
corner
escape was, at last, a reality.

Milton Keynes UK
Ingram Content Group UK Ltd.
UKHW020931110624
444053UK00015B/861

9 789358 318180